SOME THINGS NEVER CHANGE.

THE PLANE RIDES. THE PRESS CONFERENCES. THE SPEECHES.

SHAKING HANDS. REMEMBERING NAMES. HAMMERING IMPORTANT POINTS HOME.

AND IF YOU'RE LUCKY, MAYBE A FEW HOURS SLEEP.

BUT AT THE END OF THE DAY, POLITICS IS ALL ABOUT BELIEF AND TRUST.

IF THE PEOPLE TRUST YOU AND BELIEVE YOU'RE AS GOOD AS YOUR WORD...

WILLARD MITT ROMNEY WAS BORN ON MARCH 12, 1947 TO GEORGE AND LENORE ROMNEY, A RELIGIOUS, YET REAL WORLD SAVVY COUPLE.

GROWING UP, ROMNEY LEARNED AT THE FEET OF HIS FATHER; A DYNAMIC BUSINESSMAN IN THE AUTO INDUSTRY...

ROMNEY RECEIVED HIS FIRST TASTE OF POLITICS DURING HIS FATHER'S TWO TERMS AS GOVERNOR OF MICHIGAN AND AN UNSUCCESSFUL RUN FOR THE REPUBLICAN PRESIDENTIAL NOMINATION IN 1964.

ROMNEY FOR PRESIDENT

ROMNEY '64

ROMNEY DOWNPLAYED HIS LEVEL OF PRIVILEGE BY TAKING BLUE COLLAR JOBS, SUCH AS *SECURITY GUARD* AT A *CHRYSLER AUTOMOTIVE* PLANT, DURING HIS TEEN YEARS.

AT CRANBROOK SCHOOL, A BOYS PREP ACADEMY, ROMNEY WAS KNOWN FOR HIS ATHLETIC AND SOCIAL SKILLS. IT WAS NO SECRET THAT HE WAS NOT A STAR PUPIL.

DURING HIS SENIOR YEAR AT CRANBROOK, ROMNEY BEGAN DATING ANN DAVIS. BY THE END OF HIS SENIOR YEAR IN 1965, THE COUPLE HAD INFORMALLY AGREED TO MARRY.

FOLLOWING GRADUATION, HE SPENT A YEAR AT STANFORD UNIVERSITY, WHERE IN MAY 1966, HE JOINED A PROTEST AIMED AT ANTI-WAR PROTESTORS.

IN JULY 1966, ROMNEY WENT TO FRANCE TO BEGIN A 30 MONTH STINT AS A MORMON MISSIONARY. HIS INTRODUCTION TO A VERY DIFFERENT WORLD WOULD NOT BE EASY.

FOR THE FIRST TIME, ROMNEY WAS FORCED TO COME TO GRIPS WITH LIVING LIKE A POOR MAN.

HE WAS FRUSTRATED THAT THE FRENCH WERE MORE INTERESTED IN SMOKING, DRINKING AND DATING THAN HEARING THE 'GOOD WORD'.

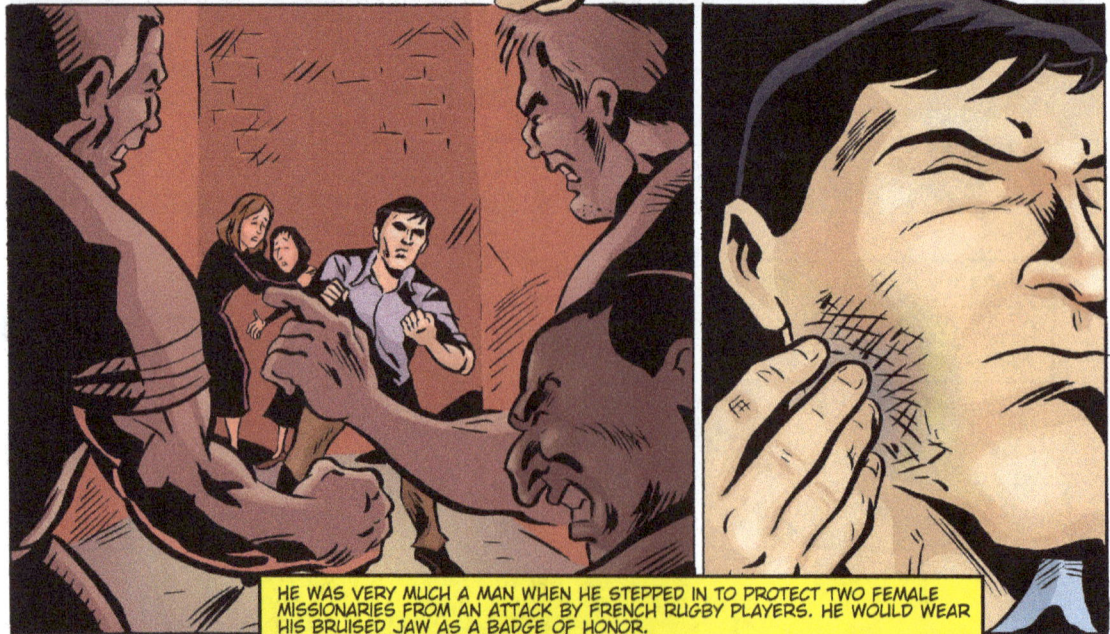

THE WAY TO GOD

HE WAS VERY MUCH A MAN WHEN HE STEPPED IN TO PROTECT TWO FEMALE MISSIONARIES FROM AN ATTACK BY FRENCH RUGBY PLAYERS. HE WOULD WEAR HIS BRUISED JAW AS A BADGE OF HONOR.

ON JUNE 16, 1968 A CAR DRIVEN BY ROMNEY WAS STRUCK HEAD ON BY ANOTHER CAR. THE WIFE OF THE MORMON MISSION PRESIDENT WAS KILLED INSTANTLY AND ROMNEY WAS RUSHED TO A NEARBY HOSPITAL IN SERIOUS CONDITION.

ROMNEY RECOVERED AND, AFTER BEING NAMED CO-ACTING PRESIDENT OF THE MISSION, SET ABOUT MOTIVATING THE DEMORALIZED MISSION MEMBERS.

UNDER HIS GUIDANCE, THE MISSION MADE GREAT STRIDES IN BRINGING THE 'WORD' TO THE FRENCH PEOPLE...

ROMNEY CHANGED. HE WAS MORE A TUNED TO THE FRAGILE NATURE OF LIFE AND A NEW FAITH IN THE SERIOUSNESS OF PURPOSE.

ROMNEY HAD TURNED THE CORNER OF DOUBT AND HALF HEARTEDNESS AND WAS NOW A FIRM BELIEVER IN THE WORD OF THE LORD.

ROMNEY RETURNED FROM HIS MISSION IN DECEMBER 1968. THREE MONTHS LATER ANNE AND HE WERE MARRIED IN A TRADITIONAL MORMON CEREMONY AT THE SALT LAKE CITY TEMPLE.

ROMNEY ENROLLED AT BRIGHAM YOUNG UNIVERSITY. BY THE TIME HE GRADUATED IN 1971, TWO CHILDREN HAD BEEN ADDED TO THE FAMILY EQUATION.

AT HIS FATHER'S SUGGESTION, ROMNEY JUMPED IMMEDIATELY INTO A JOINT LAW/BUSINESS COURSE AT HARVARD.

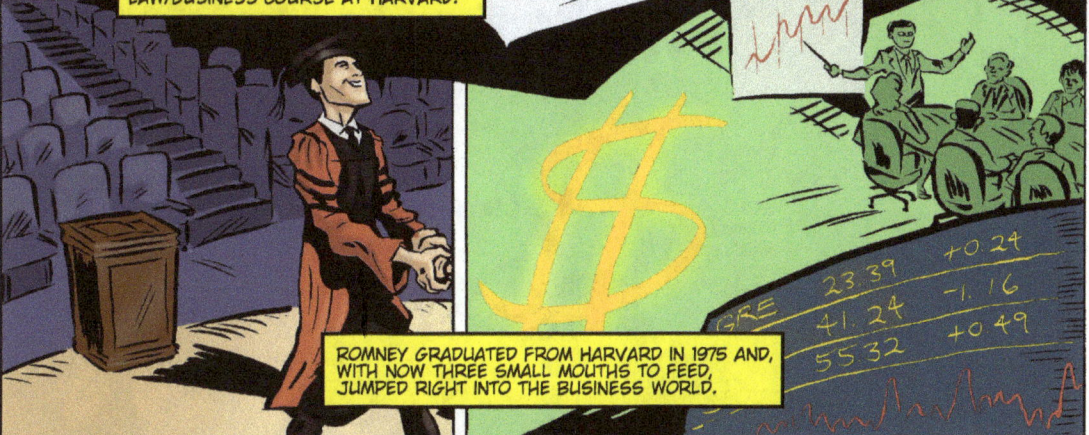

ROMNEY GRADUATED FROM HARVARD IN 1975 AND, WITH NOW THREE SMALL MOUTHS TO FEED, JUMPED RIGHT INTO THE BUSINESS WORLD.

BETWEEN 1975 AND 1994 ROMNEY MADE GREAT STRIDES IN THE BUSINESS WORLD AT SEVERAL EAST COAST BASED FIRMS...

...WITH AN APPROACH THAT EMPHASIZED BOTH HIS BUSINESS AND LAW INFLUENCES AND A PHILOSOPHICAL APPROACH THAT MADE THE OFTEN COLD HEARTED ELEMENTS OF BUSINESS MORE PERSONAL.

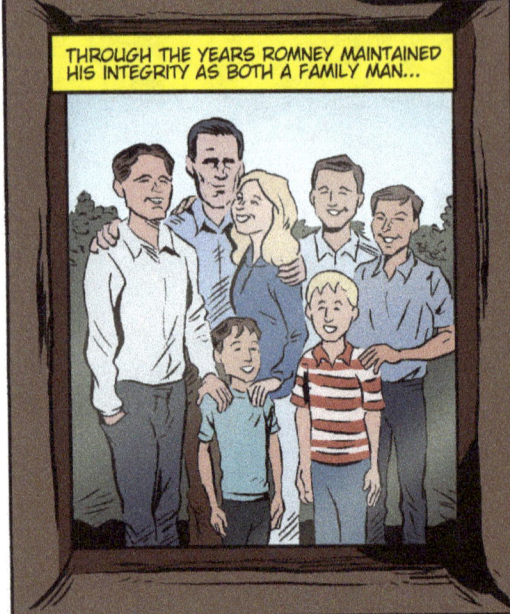

THROUGH THE YEARS ROMNEY MAINTAINED HIS INTEGRITY AS BOTH A FAMILY MAN...

...AND A COMMITTED MAN OF FAITH IN BOTH WORD AND DEED.

ROMNEY TURNED TO POLITICS IN 1994, FIRST CAPTURING THE *REPUBLICAN PRIMARY* AND THEN SQUARING OFF AGAINST INCUMBENT MASSACHUSETTS SENATOR *TED KENNEDY.*

IT WAS A SPIRITED CAMPAIGN. ROMNEY WAS OFTEN THE TARGET OF NASTY ATTACK ADS. BUT ROMNEY FOUGHT A GOOD FIGHT BEFORE ULTIMATELY LOSING TO KENNEDY IN A CLOSE RACE.

ROMNEY RETURNED TO THE BUSINESS WORLD BUT NOT BEFORE VOWING TO HIS BROTHER: "I NEVER WANT TO RUN FOR SOMETHING AGAIN UNLESS I CAN WIN."

HE TRIUMPHED OVER PERSONAL TRAGEDY WITH THE DEATH OF HIS FATHER IN 1995, HIS MOTHER IN 1998 AND HIS WIFE'S DIAGNOSIS OF MS IN 1998...

...BEFORE SINGLEHANDEDLY TURNING THE 2002 SALT LAKE CITY WINTER OLYMPICS INTO A SUCCESS AS THE HEAD OF THE SALT LAKE ORGANIZING COMMITTEE.

IN 2002 ROMNEY REENTERED POLITICS, RUNNING AS A POLITICAL "OUTSIDER" AND BEING ELECTED GOVERNOR OF MASSACHUSETTS.

ROMNEY'S FOUR YEARS AS GOVERNOR WERE MARKED BY CONSTANT CHALLENGES ON ECONOMIC AND SOCIAL ISSUE FRONTS. TAXES AND HEALTHCARE SEEMED HIS CONSTANT COMPANIONS.

ROMNEY WAS A LIGHTNING ROD OF CONTROVERSY... EXACTLY WHAT THE REPUBLICAN PARTY WAS LOOKING FOR IN A 2008 PRESIDENTIAL CANDIDATE.

ROMNEY ANNOUNCED THAT HE WOULD NOT RUN FOR REELECTION IN 2005 AND BEGAN A CROSS COUNTRY CAMPAIGN TO BUILD PARTY SUPPORT FOR A PRESIDENTIAL RUN...

...AND ON FEBRUARY 13, 2007, ROMANY FORMALLY ANNOUNCED HIS CANDIDACY FOR THE REPUBLICAN NOMINATION FOR PRESIDENT OF THE UNITED STATES.

HIS YOUTHFUL GOOD LOOKS, BUSINESS ACUMEN AND "OUTSIDER" IMAGE SERVED ROMNEY WELL DURING THE EARLY DAYS OF THE CAMPAIGN.

AND WITH A VICTORY AT AN IOWA STRAW POLL IN AUGUST 2007, ROMNEY SEEMED THE "DARK HORSE" FRONTRUNNER IN AN ALREADY HOTLY CONTESTED RACE.

HOWEVER THAT STATUS MADE ROMNEY AN IMMEDIATE TARGET FROM CANDIDATES *JOHN McCAIN* AND *MIKE HUCKABEE* WHO ATTACKED ROMNEY ON HIS RELIGIOUS IDEALS AND POLITICAL INCONSISTENCIES.

ROMNEY DEFLECTED THE ATTACKS AND CONTINUED TO WAGE A NON-STOP CAMPAIGN THAT SAW HIM CAPTURE *ELEVEN PRIMARIES* AND *CAUCUSES* AND *4.7 MILLION* VOTES.

SADLY ROMNEY CAME UP SHORT AGAINST THE MCCAIN AND ON FEBRUARY 7, 2008 HE ANNOUNCED THE END OF HIS PRESIDENTIAL RUN.

ROMNEY PROVED A TIRELESS CAMPAIGNER FOR MCCAIN IN THE WAKE OF HIS CONCESSION, APPEARING AT REPUBLICAN FUNDRAISERS AND REGULARLY ACTING AS MCCAIN'S SURROGATE ON CABLE NEWS PROGRAMS.

THE TWO POLITICIANS BECAME GOOD FRIENDS AND THE TALK WAS THAT ROMNEY WAS ON THE SHORT LIST FOR VICE PRESIDENT ALONGSIDE MCCAIN.

CONSEQUENTLY NOBODY WAS MORE SURPRISED THAN ROMNEY WHEN MCCAIN ANNOUNCED ALASKA GOVERNOR *SARAH PALIN* AS HIS RUNNING MATE.

NOT LONG AFTER JOHN MCCAIN WAS DEFEATED BY *BARACK OBAMA*, ROMNEY BEGAN TO QUIETLY RETRENCH FOR ANOTHER RUN AT THE WHITE HOUSE.

HE RAISED CAMPAIGN FUNDS AND KEPT LOYAL MEMBERS OF HIS 2008 CAMPAIGN CLOSE AT HAND.

WHEN A SPECIAL ELECTION WAS HELD TO FILL THE VACANCY LEFT BY THE DEATH OF TED KENNEDY IN 2010, ROMNEY THREW HIS EXPERTISE AND SUPPORT BEHIND THE EVENTUAL WINNER, *SCOTT BROWN*.

ROMNEY vs. SKY BLU!

ROMNEY MADE HEADLINES THAT YEAR WHEN AN ARGUMENT ON A PLANE WITH *LAMFAO* BAND MEMBER *SKY BLU* RESULTED IN A MOMENTARY SHOVING MATCH.

THE NEW YORK TIMES
BESTSELLER LIST

1 THE CASE FOR AMERICAN GREATNESS
by MITT ROMNEY

2

ROMNEY'S BOOK, *THE CASE FOR AMERICAN GREATNESS*, WAS RELEASED ON MARCH 2, 2010 AND ROCKETED TO THE TOP OF THE *NEW YORK TIMES* BEST SELLER LIST.

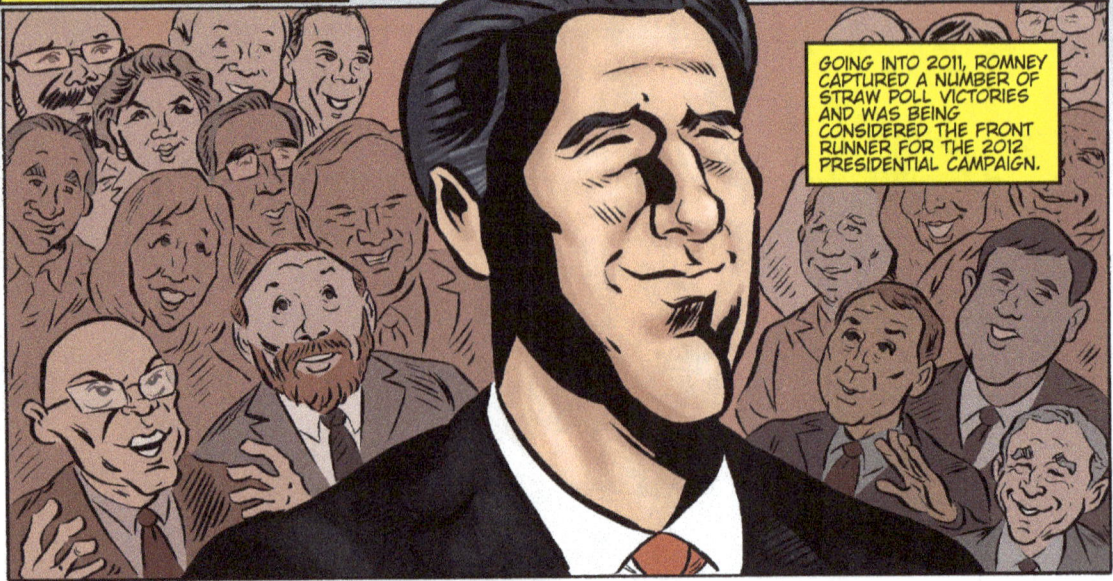

GOING INTO 2011, ROMNEY CAPTURED A NUMBER OF STRAW POLL VICTORIES AND WAS BEING CONSIDERED THE FRONT RUNNER FOR THE 2012 PRESIDENTIAL CAMPAIGN.

He teased the speculation on April 11, 2011 when he announced the formation of an exploratory committee as the first step at a second presidential run at the University of New Hampshire.

Although considered a front runner, many still questioned Romney's attitude toward healthcare reform and his history of balancing state budgets.

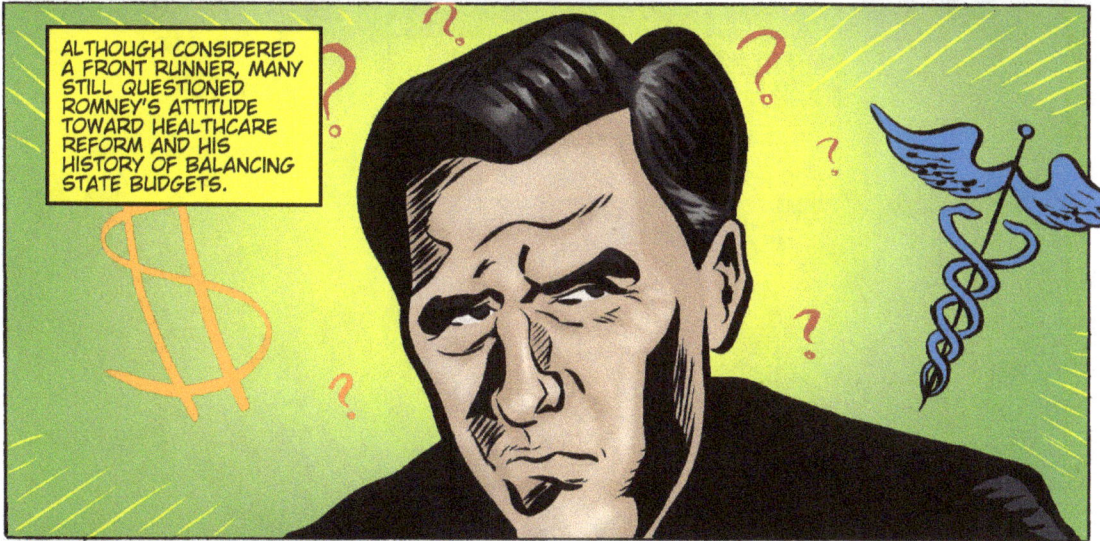

But those doubts did not prevent Romney, at a New Hampshire farm, from officially throwing his hat into the presidential race on June 2.

TWO WEEKS LATER ROMNEY WAS ON FIRE, ATTACKING THE SITTING PRESIDENT BARACK OBAMA, AND GOING TOE TO TOE WITH THE LIKES OF *RON PAUL*, *NEWT GINGRICH* AND *MICHELE BACHMANN* IN THE FIRST GOP CANDIDATES DEBATE. FOR ROMNEY, IT WAS GAME ON.

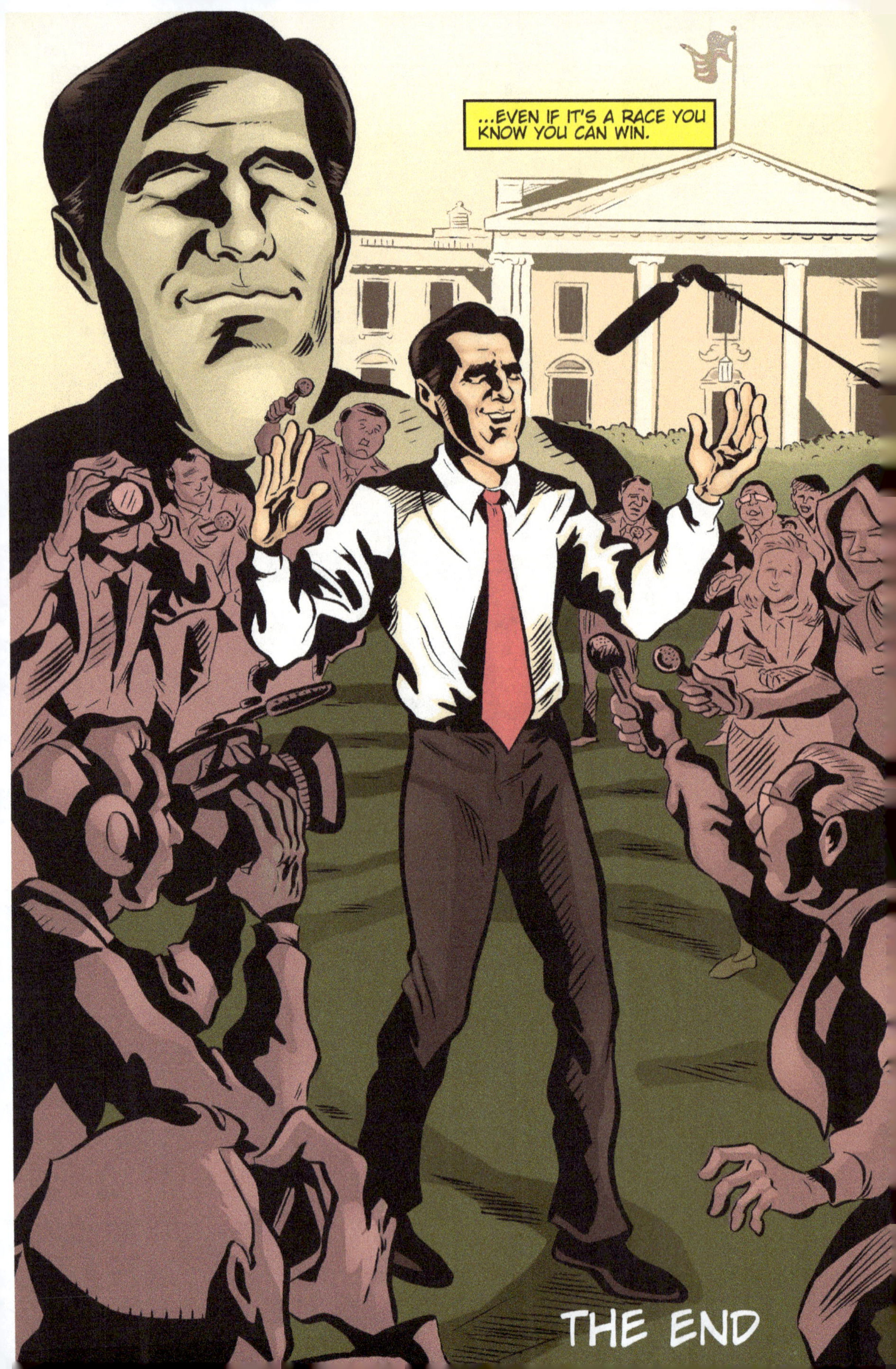
...EVEN IF IT'S A RACE YOU KNOW YOU CAN WIN.
THE END

#ERASEHATE WITH THE MATTHEW SHEPARD FOUNDATION

With your donated dollars and volunteer hours, we work tirelessly to erase hate from every corner of America through our programs.

SPEAKING ENGAGEMENTS

Since Matt's death in 1998, Judy and Dennis have been determined to prevent others from similar tragedies. By sharing their story, they are able to carry on Matt's legacy.

HATE CRIMES REPORTING

Our work to improve reporting includes conducting trainings for law enforcement agencies, building relationships between community leaders and law enforcement, and developing policy reform in reporting practices.

LARAMIE PROJECT

MSF offers support to productions of The Laramie Project, which depicts the events leading up to and after Matt's murder. It remains one of the most performed plays in America.

MATTHEW'S PLACE

MatthewsPlace.com is a blog designed to provide young LGBTQ+ people with an outlet for their voices. From finance to health to love and dating, and everything in between, our writers contribute excellent material.

Matthew Shepard Foundation
embracing diversity